REPAIRING THE DAMAGE

Pollution

Repairing the Damage

Pollution

Alan Collinson

EVANS BROTHERS LIMITED

Evans Brothers Limited
2A Portman Mansions
Chiltern Street
London W1M 1LE

First published 1991
Reprinted 1992, 1994, 1996
First published in paperback 1997

Typeset by Fleetlines Typesetters, Southend-on-Sea
Printed in Spain by GRAFO, S.A.-Bilbao

ISBN 0 237 51800 7

British Library Cataloguing in Publication Data

Collinson, Alan
    Pollution. – (Repairing the damage)
    1. Pollution – Juvenile literature
    I. Title
    363.7'3

Acknowledgements

Editor: Su Swallow
Design: Neil Sayer
Production: Jenny Mulvanny

Maps: Jillian Luff of Bitmap Graphics
Illustrations: Richard Wise

For permission to reproduce copyright material the author and
publishers gratefully acknowledge the following:

Cover (Romania) Haley, Sipa-Press/Rex Features,
Title page (Mexico City) Mark Edwards, Still Pictures **p4** Joyce
Photographics, Planet Earth Pictures **p5** (top) David Reed,
Panos Pictures, (bottom) Sebastiao Salgado, Jr, Magnum **p8**
Mary Evans Picture Library **p9** (top) Ardea London Ltd **p10**
Tony Craddock, Science Photo Library **p11** Ardea London Ltd,
(inset) Lawrence Migdale, Science Photo Library **p12** Fred
Mayer, Magnum **p13** (top) The Hulton-Deutsch Collection,
(bottom) Burt Glinn, Magnum **p16** (top) Will McIntyre, Science
Photo Library, (bottom) Pierre Schwartz, Sipa-Press/Rex
Features **p17** Adam Hart Davies, Science Photo Library
p18 Joel Bennett, Survival Anglia **p19** (top) Greenwood/
ECOSCENE, (bottom) Rapho, Berretty, Science Photo Library
p20 Alan Collinson **p21** (top) Mark Edwards, Still Pictures,
(others) Alan Collinson **p23** Novosti/Science Photo Library
p24 Novosti/Science Photo Library **p26** Rasmussen, Sipa-Press/
Rex Features **p28** US Dept of Energy/Science Photo Library
p29 (left) e.t. archive, (right) US Dept of Energy, Science Photo
Library **p30** Philipe Plailly, Science Photo Library **p31** Alan
Collinson **p32** (top) Adam Hart-Davis, Science Photo Library,
(bottom) Anthony and Elizabeth Bomford, Ardea London Ltd
p33 Ron Giling, Panos Pictures **p34** Robert Harding Picture
Library **p35** Michael Martin, Science Photo Library **p36** Peter
Menzel, Science Photo Library **p37** David Scharf, Science Photo
Library **p38** Warren Willaims, Planet Earth Pictures, (inset) Dr
Fred Espenak, Science Photo Library **p39** (left) Ian Beames,
Ardea London Ltd, (right) Mark Edwards, Still Pictures **p40** Dr
Gene Feldman, NASA GSFC/Science Photo Library **p41** Hank
Morgan, Science Photo Library **p43** NASA/Science Photo Library

CONTENTS

INTRODUCTION

Pollution means the spoiling of a healthy and balanced environment by adding substances to it. These substances (pollutants) may be completely new to the environment, or they may be present naturally. Chemicals such as nitrates for example, may be present naturally as a plant food but they become a pollutant in fertilisers which are added to the soil in large amounts. Other chemicals used to kill pests and weeds may help crops to grow but they also kill many non-harmful insects and plants living in the same environment as the crops. Pollutants such as rubbish dumped on the land, oil spilled at sea and gases produced by burning fossil fuels (coal, oil and gas) also spoil the environment.

Some environments can seem very clean and unspoilt. It is hard to imagine, for instance, that the Sahara Desert or the Antarctic are not clean. But this impression of cleanliness is an illusion. In fact there are no environments left on Earth which are not polluted to some extent. Our industries, farming, transport systems and even our own homes add pollutants to the Earth's atmosphere and seas. The air and water carry our pollutants to all corners of the Earth.

Chain of events

Today it would be difficult to ignore all the television and newspaper reports of pollution and its dangers. Yet 40 years ago few people were aware of the problem, although it did exist. However, some scientists were beginning to worry about pollution – not only the obvious kinds such as smog and smoke, but the less visible forms, too. As industry produced more and added more chemicals to the environment, scientists noticed some alarming signs that all was not well. In 1962 an American scientist, Rachel Carson, wrote a book called *Silent Spring*. The book set out very clearly the effects that pesticides were having on the animal populations of America. Birds of prey were disappearing from their territories, often far from farmlands where chemicals were being sprayed. Rachel Carson found that these animals were being poisoned by the chemicals, especially one chemical named DDT which killed insects very effectively. The chemical passed from soil to plant to small animals and finally to birds such as hawks, owls, eagles, and some sea birds. Each time DDT passed along the links in the food chain it became more concentrated. Eventually it was so concentrated in the flesh-eating birds that it interfered with such things as eggshell formation. The shells of the eggs were so thin that the birds crushed them as they tried to incubate them. Fewer young were produced and in many areas owls, hawks and other birds of prey disappeared.

Rubbish is now spoiling Antarctica at scientific bases and, in the sea, poisonous chemicals are affecting wildlife.

At first the chemical industries denied that the pesticide was dangerous. But when DDT was discovered in human mothers' milk in many parts of Europe and America, even in mothers who lived as far away from farmland as the Arctic, the general public joined in the protests and DDT was eventually banned in the rich countries. (In the poor countries, however, it is still used sometimes. Here, protecting people from the deadly diseases carried by mosquitoes is considered more important than preventing pollution.)

Science was able to follow the path of DDT from one creature to another because of the growth in the science of ECOLOGY. This science deals with the relationships between animals and plants and the environments in which they live. Understanding these relationships can help us to repair the damage we do. As you will see in this book, many people around the world are working actively to rebuild a less polluted world. But there are no easy answers. To achieve the goal of a cleaner world will take the efforts of all of us, not just of the scientists. If we are not prepared to make the effort, no amount of knowledge will help us.

Pollution of the Earth began with prehistoric hunters and farmers (see page 6).

Mexico City is one of the most polluted cities in the world, yet thousands of people arrive there every day from the countryside looking for work.

CHAPTER ONE

SPOILING SPACESHIP EARTH

Stone Age pollution

Fossils and genes suggest that people like us developed from earlier humans about 200,000 years ago in Africa. From their original home, probably in Africa, they spread gradually around the world. They seem to have reached North America, for example, about 30,000 years ago, by walking across from Asia into Alaska. (Of course, this land is now drowned under the waters of the Bering Strait but then, in the Ice Age, it was dry land. The sea level was lower because vast quantities of water were locked up in huge ice sheets.)

These early people gathered and hunted their food and used only simple tools made of stone. As there were so few people alive in the Old Stone Age, the change they brought about in the Earth's environment as a whole was not great. But even these few people – possibly as few as one million – produced some changes. For example, by lighting fires they destroyed forests and caused the spread of grassland. By hunting the huge creatures which roamed the forests and grasslands of North America they reduced the numbers of animals. In fact, they may even have driven these enormous creatures to extinction.

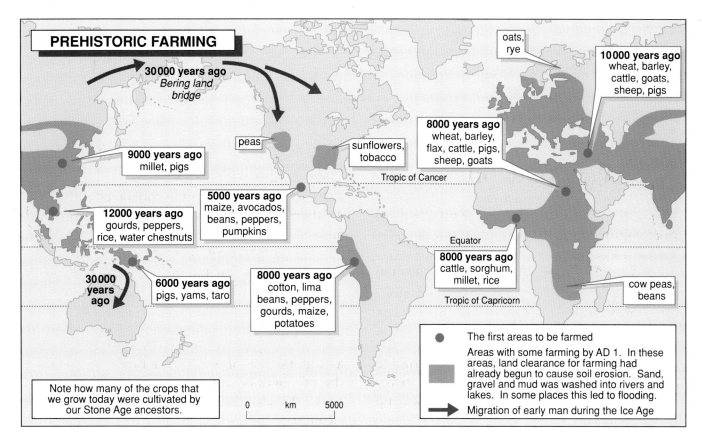

PREHISTORIC FARMING

30 000 years ago
Bering land bridge

oats, rye

10 000 years ago
wheat, barley, cattle, goats, sheep, pigs

peas

9000 years ago
millet, pigs

sunflowers, tobacco

8000 years ago
wheat, barley, flax, cattle, pigs, sheep, goats

Tropic of Cancer

5000 years ago
maize, avocados, beans, peppers, pumpkins

12000 years ago
gourds, peppers, rice, water chestnuts

Equator

8000 years ago
cattle, sorghum, millet, rice

30 000 years ago

6000 years ago
pigs, yams, taro

8000 years ago
cotton, lima beans, peppers, gourds, maize, potatoes

cow peas, beans

Tropic of Capricorn

● The first areas to be farmed

Areas with some farming by AD 1. In these areas, land clearance for farming had already begun to cause soil erosion. Sand, gravel and mud was washed into rivers and lakes. In some places this led to flooding.

➡ Migration of early man during the Ice Age

Note how many of the crops that we grow today were cultivated by our Stone Age ancestors.

0   km   5000

The people of the Old Stone Age did not produce large-scale pollution, but they did begin to alter the balances in nature between plants and animals and their environments.

Pollution and disease

About 12,000 years ago this situation began to change. For the first time people learned how to farm crops instead of hunting and gathering their food. This is named the Agricultural Revolution. People settled in villages and, later, in towns in Asia and Europe, then in Central and South America. Wastes such as sewage began to pollute the environment. This led to the spread of diseases. Leprosy, smallpox, plague, typhoid and cholera spread as water supplies became polluted by human wastes. Rats, fleas and other vermin made their home in the towns and helped to spread these diseases. This was the beginning of the age of pollution. There is even evidence that some towns had to be abandoned as the population was affected by epidemics of disease. However, even though pollution at this

In the New Stone Age, burning forests and growing crops altered large areas of land in many parts of the world.

time was a serious problem in certain places, the total amount worldwide was fairly small, and as yet few non-natural materials had been added to the environment.

Mine wastes

About 5000 years ago, in Europe and Asia at first and later in Africa and Central and South America, people discovered how to heat certain kinds of rock to extract metals. (This is named smelting.) Copper, then bronze (tin and copper) and finally iron were used to make more efficient tools and weapons. Silver and gold were also mined and smelted as in ancient Athens. Trade and shipping grew but the debris from mining and smelting was dumped on the land. Mine wastes, often highly poisonous, began to affect rivers and streams. At the same time, large areas of forest were cut down to provide the charcoal (baked wood) for the smelting, so hills in areas such as the eastern Mediterranean and the Middle East began to lose their forests. As a result soils were washed away and dumped on the lower parts of valleys. Floods became more frequent as the run-off from storms was not trapped by the forests.

There were a few attempts to repair the increasing damage and control the destruction of land by mining. One such attempt was made in Germany in the Middle Ages. In some small states with large mineral deposits, the miners were given licences to extract the minerals and smelt them, provided they restored the land afterwards and buried the wastes. They also had to plant trees to replace any they cut down to make charcoal.

Other kinds of pollution also began to appear. For example, by the thirteenth century coal was being widely used in Britain to heat houses in towns. (It was not used to provide power or to smelt metals.) The pollution from coal smoke became so bad that in the reign of Edward I (1272–1307) and again in Queen Elizabeth I's reign (1558–1603) laws were passed against burning coal in London. As coal was so cheap, nobody took much notice. Coal smoke pollution continued to increase until the 1950s, when the Clean Air Acts came into force in 1958 (see page 12).

John Evelyn was an early campaigner against pollution.

New power, new pollution

In the seventeenth century, an Englishman, John Evelyn, produced two books on pollution and the destruction of the environment. The first was a plan to solve the smoke pollution problem of London, the second was a plan to save the English woodlands. But before his ideas could be fully tested, a major change took place which destroyed any hope of controlling pollution for many years to come. In Coalbrookedale in the English Midlands, a man called Abraham Darby discovered how to use coal turned into coke to smelt iron ore. From the middle of the eighteenth century the use of coke spread rapidly and reduced the demand for wood. Coal was also soon providing steam power for engines. By 1800 the Industrial Revolution was fully under way. These developments were carried abroad, first to Belgium where an iron works was founded in Liège.

The Industrial Revolution spread as railways grew and by 1850 was well under way in northern Europe and in northeast USA. But the Industrial Revolution was also a pollution revolution. Large quantities of minerals – metal ores, coal, and later oil and gas – were extracted from the Earth. The waste products of the

industries using these minerals poured on to the land, into the rivers and into the air. Products were introduced into the environment which had no similarities to the natural materials with which Nature could cope.

Of course, people's standard of living, measured in the goods and services they could buy, grew. But the warnings which John Evelyn had given about the destruction of the environment were largely forgotten.

Town plans

By the end of the nineteenth century the great cities of the industrial countries had become badly disorganised. Many poor people who had left the countryside to work in the new factories were packed into slums in the most polluted parts of the towns. Many young children died and adults suffered from frequent illness caused by the polluted air and bad drains. At this time, architects and planners began to look for ways to improve people's living conditions.

In the 1820s, smoke polluted the air at coal mine pitheads.

In the 1920s, French architect Le Corbusier planned a town of tower blocks and open spaces, without any industry.

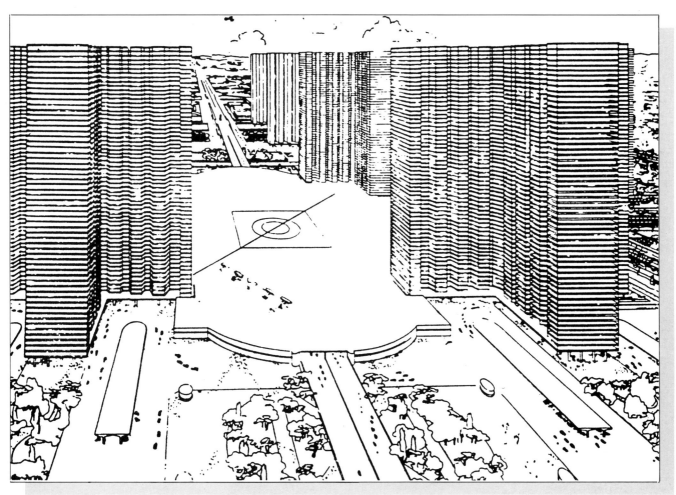

In Britain, Ebenezer Howard suggested people should escape from the cities altogether and live in 'garden cities' to be built in the countryside. In France, Tony Garnier suggested that all industry should be pushed out of cities into special zones away from people's homes. In Italy, a group of artists and architects (the Futurists) suggested that the old cities of Europe should be torn down altogether. The cities should be rebuilt in modern materials such as reinforced concrete, with wide streets, tower blocks and plenty of public open space away from industry. As the twentieth century progressed, many of these ideas were adopted in Europe and North America.

All these changes created our modern townscapes. They improved peoples' lives, but they did not tackle the underlying causes of pollution. Chemicals and other wastes continued to be produced in increasing amounts. New kinds of pollution appeared, such as that from vehicle exhausts. Chemicals in the form of herbicides (to kill weeds) and pesticides were used in industrialised farming. New forms of power were developed – atomic power and hydro-

electricity, for example – which presented new pollution problems, and so on. It is important to remember that although many people in the developed countries now live in clean towns, mostly in homes with clean water and good drains, the pollution they cause is pushed out into the whole world environment. Between 80 per cent and 90 per cent of all the world's polluting chemicals are produced in these countries. The developing countries produce very little pollution – so far!

The Age of Conservation

A hundred years ago, it was the architects and planners who provided the solutions to the

In Germany, open cast mining of brown coal – the dirtiest fuel in industry – produces great scars on the land (below). Eventually, this machine (right) puts back the earth, which is then planted with crops. The first crop is lucerne (see page 11).

pollution problems as they saw them. Now it is the scientists, the engineers and the public at large who have seen the problems and who will have to provide the solutions. Everyone agrees that solutions have to be found quickly. Nature can only take so much damage. We can no longer expect the natural world to absorb all our rubbish. Eventually, the life support systems of our spaceship Earth will buckle under the pressure and we will be destroyed with it. Nature needs our help to conserve the Earth. Happily there are now many signs that the new Age of Conservation has begun.

Lucerne is often used to restore polluted land. Its long roots help to bring nutrients to the surface, so that other plants can grow. Scientists can alter plants (inset) so that they will grow easily on polluted soil.

Giving Nature a hand

Nature can often adapt, given enough time, to deal with pollution. Over many years plants change so that they can grow in the polluted environment. But this is a very slow process. The pollution created by people is produced so quickly that Nature finds it hard to adapt quickly enough.

Now, scientists have taken plants that are known to be adaptable and improved them by breeding and genetic engineering so that the process of colonisation is speeded up. This kind of research means that in future Nature can be helped in its ability to heal the effects of pollution of the environment.

CHAPTER TWO

TURNING POINTS

During the last few decades some events – oil spills, nuclear accidents and other less dramatic events – have caused people to take a close look at what is happening to our environment. Many of them have resulted in important changes in the way we do things. (See chart on page 14.) They are turning points on the road towards repairing the damage from pollution and preventing it in future.

Unfortunately, some of these turning points have only been taken because people suffered in large numbers and showed up what was wrong. For example, in 1984 an accident at a chemical factory in Bhopal in India directly killed 3300 people. It seriously injured between 100,000 and 250,000 people, and at least 200,000 were affected in less serious ways. Compensation from the American company that owned the plant totalled 440 million dollars. If an accident of this scale had happened in a rich country, the company would have had to pay much more and would probably have collapsed. Under American law the people who ran the company could well have gone to jail.

At about the same time, it was realised that many companies were dumping toxic waste produced in the rich countries in poor ones such as Nigeria and other West African states. However, in 1994 the island countries of the South-West Pacific agreed to ban dumping on their land and nearby seas. Most of the wastes were coming from the USA.

The Indian government is now also stricter about the kinds of industries that foreign countries set up there. Industrial companies are being forced to clean up their production methods to make them safe for everybody, rich and poor. This will cost money. People who use the products of industry will all have to share in these extra costs. So far we have had cheap goods at the expense of other people – and the planet itself.

There will be many other turning points ahead like these before we are fully in charge of the conservation of our planet. The turning points are not always sharp. Often a turn away from pollution leads to another problem which itself becomes a turning point as it is solved.

A new turn

Smog is a mixture of smoke, fog, and chemical fumes. Smogs were once common in London, but the worst was in December 1952 (see page 13). The results of that smog were so bad that it became a turning point: cleaning up the air became an urgent task for the government. More than 2000 people had died as a result of the smog, mostly the old or people with asthma or bronchitis and small children with breathing problems. Many more old people had suffered permanent damage to their lungs.

The first Clean Air Act limited the use of open coal fires and open rubbish fires. Bronchitis and asthma, in children especially, declined. Soon the palls of smoke which had been a feature of British towns since the Industrial Revolution began to disappear.

Pittsburgh, USA was one of the first major industrial towns in Europe and the USA in which pollution was brought under control.

The Great London Smog

The author of this book remembers the worst smog in London:

'In 1952 I was a student in London. The morning of December 5 had been fine and clear, sunny but cold. About two o'clock in the afternoon I was looking out of the window over the Thames during a rather boring lecture when I noticed a strong dark line had appeared across the sky. I had never seen anything like it before. Gradually, over the next hour it began to get dark. What looked like smoke began to curl into the room through an open window. It smelled strongly of coal smoke. At first we thought it was just one of the 'standard' London fogs we were used to – we called them 'pea-soupers' – but it soon proved more than that.

That evening I went to the cinema. By the second film, the haze was so thick that the few people left in the cinema had to move down to the front seats to see the film properly.

The next day the fog became even thicker. Street lights were no help at all. Gradually traffic disappeared. London became a silent, dead city. It was at this stage that the fog began to change. The grey thick mist turned yellow and began to smell, or rather taste, very bad. Breathing in was likely to produce a sharp pain in the lungs and if you were suffering from a cold then you could expect a terrible cough, with no fresh air anywhere. In fact, we were breathing in sulphuric acid. We used our college scarves as fog masks.

By Saturday all the buses had stopped, even though they had tried to keep them running by the conductor walking in front with a mercury flare to guide the driver. He also carried a stick to feel for the edge of the road. Remember, this was in the daytime, not at night. Only the underground trains were keeping the city moving.

When the fog finally began to lift, on the following Tuesday, a really strange sight was revealed. The common opposite our house was strewn with cars, lorries and buses. One or two had even gone into the duck ponds. There were stories of drivers wandering around for hours trying to find their way off the common. We all knew we had experienced something quite extraordinary. It was like being marooned in Space; the rest of the planet seemed to have disappeared. I hope nobody ever experiences anything like it again.'

December 1952: a London bus was led through the fog by an inspector carrying a flare. This was daylight.

On the road to a cleaner future?

These are some of the most important turning points of the past 50 years on the road to a cleaner world. Without them, the road would have led to the 'Age of Pollution', not the 'Age of Conservation'. Although pollution has increased, there have been so many serious incidents in the last decade that we have been forced to take drastic and long-lasting action.

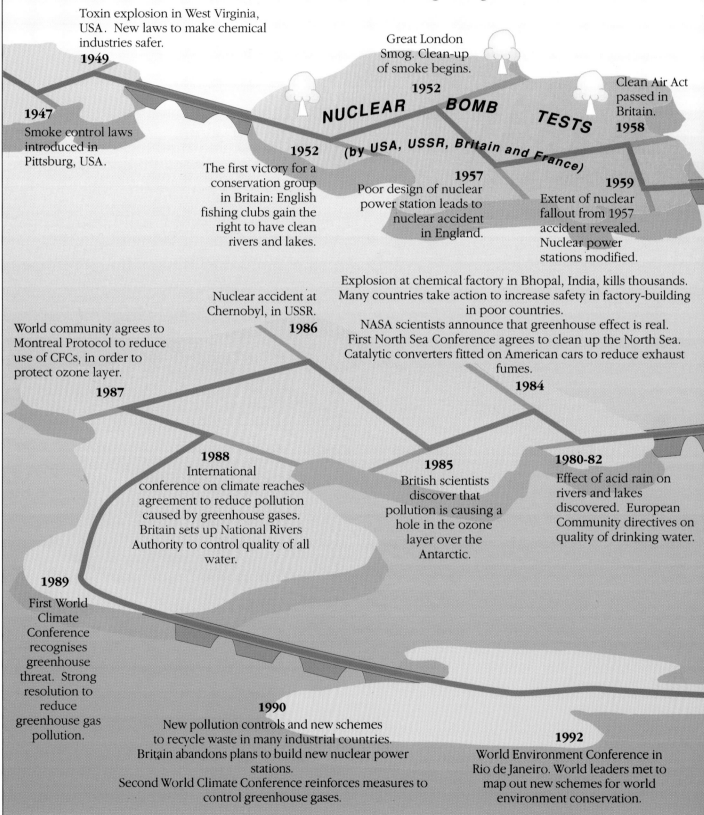

Toxin explosion in West Virginia, USA. New laws to make chemical industries safer.
1949

Great London Smog. Clean-up of smoke begins.
1952

Clean Air Act passed in Britain.
1958

1947
Smoke control laws introduced in Pittsburg, USA.

NUCLEAR BOMB TESTS
(by USA, USSR, Britain and France)

1952
The first victory for a conservation group in Britain: English fishing clubs gain the right to have clean rivers and lakes.

1957
Poor design of nuclear power station leads to nuclear accident in England.

1959
Extent of nuclear fallout from 1957 accident revealed. Nuclear power stations modified.

Nuclear accident at Chernobyl, in USSR.
1986

Explosion at chemical factory in Bhopal, India, kills thousands. Many countries take action to increase safety in factory-building in poor countries.
NASA scientists announce that greenhouse effect is real.
First North Sea Conference agrees to clean up the North Sea.
Catalytic converters fitted on American cars to reduce exhaust fumes.
1984

World community agrees to Montreal Protocol to reduce use of CFCs, in order to protect ozone layer.
1987

1988
International conference on climate reaches agreement to reduce pollution caused by greenhouse gases. Britain sets up National Rivers Authority to control quality of all water.

1985
British scientists discover that pollution is causing a hole in the ozone layer over the Antarctic.

1980-82
Effect of acid rain on rivers and lakes discovered. European Community directives on quality of drinking water.

1989
First World Climate Conference recognises greenhouse threat. Strong resolution to reduce greenhouse gas pollution.

1990
New pollution controls and new schemes to recycle waste in many industrial countries. Britain abandons plans to build new nuclear power stations. Second World Climate Conference reinforces measures to control greenhouse gases.

1992
World Environment Conference in Rio de Janeiro. World leaders met to map out new schemes for world environment conservation.

When the Cold War ended in 1989-1990, the extent of pollution in eastern Europe, including the USSR, was finally revealed. To reach a cleaner world in the twenty-first century the industries of eastern Europe will have to invest effort and money to match the standards now being imposed in western Europe, USA, Canada and Japan.

Nuclear Test Ban treaty signed by USA, USSR and Britain. Ban stops most tests above ground.
1963

International group called Club of Rome produces influential report showing that pollution will increase if industry grows without making changes in production methods.
1969

NUCLEAR BOMB TESTS
(by China and India)

1962
Silent Spring published. Bans imposed on some agricultural chemicals in USA and Europe.

1967
Canada controls inland water pollution and Canada and USA set up commission on the Great Lakes and St Lawrence River pollution.

Three Mile Island nuclear accident forces USA to abandon nuclear power. Sweden also abandons nuclear power. Houses in USA discovered to have been built on worst toxic waste dump in the country. Strict regulations on dumping introduced.
1979

European Community directives on quality of water for swimming.
1976

UK Control of Pollution Act passed.
1974

Computer-based forecast *Limits to Growth*, published in USA, confirms link between industrial growth and pollution.
1972

1970
Environmental Protection Agency founded in the USA. Royal Commission on Environmental Pollution set up in Britain. Great public interest in pollution matters.

1973
First oil shock as price triples in one year. Many energy-saving measures introduced in USA, Europe and Japan, which reduce pollution.

1978
Second oil shock as price increases. New energy-saving measures introduced.

1975
Mediterranean Action Plan by countries bordering the sea to control pollution.

2000
Will this new millenium mark the beginning of the Age of Conservation? Many scientific and government organisations are now tackling the main problems of pollution worldwide. However it is not a straight road to a green future. Major natural disasters and wars may create new turning points.

1995–6
A pause on the road to a cleaner future as France restarts nuclear testing underground. Worldwide protests at this.

An acid test for conservation

Once domestic coal smoke had been brought under control, the major use of coal in Britain was for power generation. To get rid of the smoke from power stations, tall chimneys were built. These chimneys let the hot plume of smoke rise high enough for it to be carried off and dispersed by the wind. Any solid particles would fall out over a wide area. However, the gases in the smoke do not fall out. They are added to the upper air and dissolve in cloud droplets. Cloud droplets are already slightly acid from normal gases dissolved in them, but the smoke gases – especially sulphur dioxide – make them even more acid. Eventually, when the cloud droplets join together to make rain-drops, acid rain forms.

Other countries such as Germany, Belgium and Holland followed the British lead and built high chimneys. For a decade or so through the 1960s and into the 1970s these countries

Acid rain has severely damaged conifer trees in a forest in North Carolina, USA.

A tyre factory in Copsa, Romania, fills the air with soot and toxic gases which affect people and animals.

A new threat from the air

In Britain at the end of the 1980s doctors began to notice that the number of children with asthma was increasing once again. Instead of occurring in winter as it had before, the peak for attacks was now in summer. In California, childhood asthma in Los Angeles also shows a peak in summer. Here, the daily unbroken sunshine acts on car fumes to produce a smog no less deadly than the smoky fogs of an older Britain. The sunlight causes many of the chemicals produced by car exhausts to undergo reactions and generate new chemicals in the air. This is named photochemical smog.

One of the most dangerous of these gases is ozone, an altered form of oxygen. This invisible, poisonous gas is known to produce onsets of asthma attacks. When the smog is worst in Los Angeles, warnings are issued to people with breathing or heart problems to stay indoors. Usually these warnings are given on more than 100 days a year. Doctors in Britain now suspect that it is the sunny summers of the 1980s and 1990s, together with an increase in car fumes, which is producing the asthma increase. (The sunny summers may themselves be the product of pollution of the air by greenhouse gases. See page 41.) In 1994 American scientists announced that as many as 10,000 people in Britain and 60,000 in the USA with poor breathing may be killed annually by tiny particles of dirt from diesel vehicle exhausts.

Another step forward

In 1994 27 centres around the world which check the state of the air all agreed that, for the first time in 30 years, the atmosphere had got slightly cleaner. Polluting gases, much of them from power production, like carbon monoxide, methane, carbon dioxide and nitrous oxide declined. Nobody knows why this happened and it has since got further polluted but to try to improve the atmosphere again many countries are developing new kinds of power sources such as the Sun, waves, tides, hot rocks and the wind.

The outer rings of this tree trunk are very narrow. They show that the tree's growth has been stunted over the last 20 years of its life, probably by acid rain.

thought they had passed the turning point to a cleaner world. However, in the 1970s some disturbing observations were made in the Scandinavian countries. Lakes and rivers began to lose their fish, and trees began to die. Investigation showed that the fresh water and the soils were becoming too acid to support life. The industrial countries had simply exported their dirty air to Norway and Sweden.

In 1987 the western European industrial countries finally agreed to take measures to get rid of the sulphur dioxide by cleaning up the smoke before it is released. This will be very costly and will take a long time.

It will be even more costly to clean the smoke in eastern Europe. Former East Germany, Poland, Czechoslovakia and the USSR are even worse polluters than the western European countries. Fortunately, the end of the Cold War means that they can join western Europe on the road to a cleaner environment.

CHAPTER THREE

TROUBLED WATERS

The map opposite shows the areas of the world which are in special danger from oil pollution. This kind of pollution is caused in a number of ways. Oil may be spilled by accident when tankers are being loaded and unloaded. Between 1974 and 1990 there were 157 spills in tropical seas from offshore wells and tankers, many near delicate coral reefs and mangroves. Mining also pollutes the sea bed with the material which is used to lubricate drills as they cut into the rock to make boreholes. The bed of the North Sea has been polluted by this material, which affects marine life on the sea bed.

Oil may also be spilled from a ship damaged by bad weather, although most vessels are designed to stand up to even the worst storms, so these accidents are rare. In fact, most oil pollution is caused either deliberately or by sheer carelessness, bad seamanship or poor ship design. For example, a ship's captain sometimes orders the crew to clean out the tanks of an empty tanker at sea, using sea water. This is illegal, but saves time in port so the ship can go on to make more money. The companies which own the ships often turn a blind eye to this practice, and it is very difficult to prove in court later. In the 1988 *Exxon Valdez* disaster, for example, seamanship, ship design and profit all played a part. The hull of the tanker was ripped open on a shallow reef because the captain and others in the crew were drunk. The ship was badly designed as it only had one skin on its hull. Most tankers have two skins so that if the outer one is torn, the inner one will keep the oil

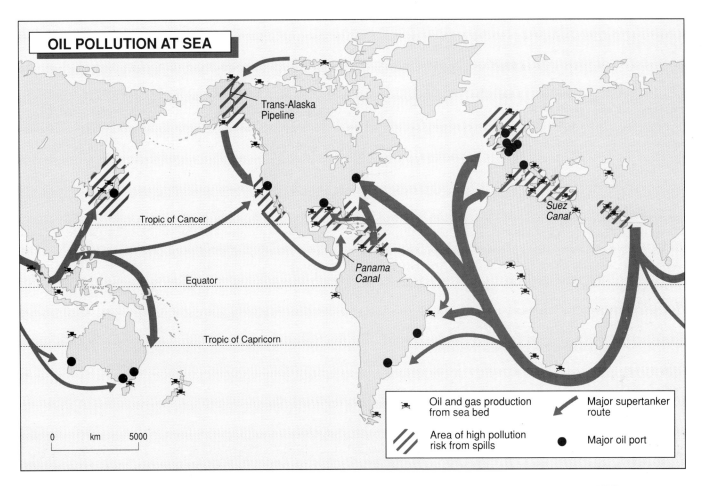

OIL POLLUTION AT SEA

Trans-Alaska Pipeline

Tropic of Cancer

Suez Canal

Equator

Panama Canal

Tropic of Capricorn

Oil and gas production from sea bed

Area of high pollution risk from spills

Major supertanker route

Major oil port

0   km   5000

in. The contents of the ruptured tanks poured into the water of Prince William Sound, ruining one of the most unspoilt natural areas on Earth. Although the company spent much money trying to clean up the mess, and the captain was prosecuted, the *Exxon Valdez* is now operating in another part of the world, still a potential disaster carrier! Only really strong laws which hurt the profits of large oil companies will keep oil pollution under control. So far developed countries where oil companies are located have done little to make the oil polluters pay.

There have been other major oil pollution events since then. In 1991 during the Gulf War, the Gulf sea was deliberately polluted with huge quantities of oil by Iraq. In 1992 in Spain, in 1993 in Scotland and in 1996 in South Wales, tankers were wrecked spilling almost as much oil as from the *Exxon Valdez*. Unfortunately, there will be more like these in the future.

At sea (left), an inflatable boom can be used to trap spilled oil until it can be removed.

Sea birds coated in oil (top right) can rarely be rescued.

Cleaning oil from a beach (bottom right) is still best done by hand.

River check

The River Tees in northeast England, 180km long, is typical of many rivers in industrial Europe and North America. Clean water is a valuable resource, so it is stored in reservoirs in the upper part of the valley for use by towns and industries downriver. The waste water is then poured back into the river, polluting its lower reaches. There is also a risk of pollution accidents from industries along its banks. Fortunately, river authorities in many industrial countries are now much more aware of the dangers of pollution and efforts are being made to clean up the worst effects.

Water from the reservoir is used to top up the river so that water can be taken from it downstream. When the reservoir was built, it destroyed the most important area of rare alpine plants in Britain. The blue gentian (below) was one of the flowers to be affected.

In 1984 chemicals from this quarry leaked into the river and killed all the fish and other wildlife for 50km downstream. The bridge in the foreground carries the Pennine Way long-distance walk.

Beauty spots such as High Force Waterfall attract many visitors. Their trampling erodes the river banks and rubbish pollutes the water.

Peat on the moors colours the water, not pollution. Salmon have returned to the river after a long absence when the water was too polluted.

Farm waste pollutes the river in summer when the water is low.

Barnard Castle

Blue gentian (see above)

A river in Italy

The River Po is fed partly by clean water from the mountains around it. Water is taken from the river for irrigation, industrial use and for drinking. But the river is polluted by industrial and farming waste and by domestic sewage. In some places, plants growing in the river take up some of the wastes and so help to clean the water. Other stretches of the river are so heavily polluted that special treatment is needed to clean it.

Polluted water

Clean water

The chemical, oil, steel and other works near the mouth of the Tees help to make the river mouth one of the most polluted in Europe.

Waste water from Darlington is poured into the River Skerne (on the right), which pollutes the otherwise clean water of the Tees (left) where the rivers join.

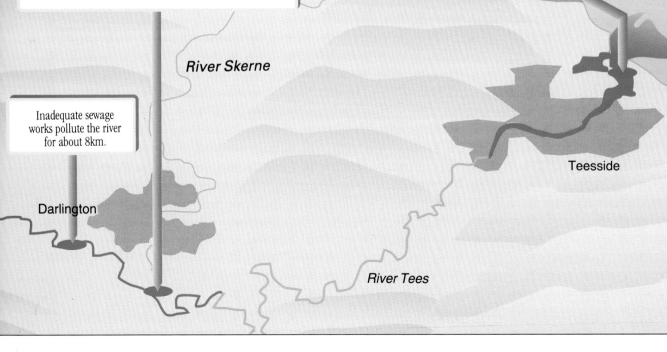

River Skerne

Inadequate sewage works pollute the river for about 8km.

Darlington

Teesside

River Tees

CHAPTER FOUR

NUCLEAR DISASTER

At 1.30am on Friday 25 April 1986 an accident occured at the Chernobyl nuclear power plant in the Ukraine, then in the USSR. Here is how one operator saw it:

'At the time of the explosion I was in a control room at the duty man's post. Suddenly, I heard a strong discharge of steam. We attached no importance to it because a discharge of steam had taken place a number of times since I have been working there. I was about to go off duty and there was an explosion. I rushed to the window. The explosion was followed instantly by further explosions. I saw a black fireball rising over the roof of the turbine building.'

This worker had just witnessed the world's most dangerous accident ever. From the reactor which had blown up many kilos of the most deadly substances in the world had been released into the environment – far more, for example than is released by the explosion of a hydrogen bomb. Yet this mass came from a plant whose technology was supposed to be absolutely safe. How could it happen?

Dangerous experiment

On Thursday 24 April operators at the nuclear power station in Chernobyl began an experiment on one of the four 1000 megawatt generators in the plant. The generators were fed by steam created by the heat generated in the nuclear reactor. To do the experiment, the operators switched off the emergency water cooling system to the reactor. Nobody switched it back on again! This was the first of six major breaches of safety that the operators committed in the run-up to the final explosion.

The Russian reactors were known to have a fault in their design from the beginning. This fault was that if the power output dropped to under 20 per cent of normal without the reactor being cooled, there would be a huge surge of steam. The operators continued with the experiment, overriding one safety system after another, even though there was this danger. At the last minute, at 1.22am, a computer printed out a mass of figures showing that the reactor was in danger of overheating. If nothing was done there would be a huge surge of steam. Nobody noticed the warning.

By this time many of the rods which cooled the reactor core had been removed. It was only at the last moment that the operators realised the danger. In panic they dropped the control rods back into the overheated core, but it was too late. The 1661 red-hot uranium rods disintegrated and broke from their metal containers to mix with the steam. The explosions which followed were huge. The exploding materials broke through the floor, walls and roof of the reactor building.

The scale of the blast was so huge it lifted off the reactor roof shield completely. This was made of 1000 tonnes of steel filled with concrete 17 metres across and three metres thick. It fell back into the reactor, breaking up the uranium rods and graphite control rods which began to burn fiercely. The fire immediately spewed out enormous quantities of deadly radioactive smoke. (Incredibly, the other reactors and generators were not shut down and continued producing power as though nothing had happened for hours afterwards.) The experiment which had ended so disastrously was actually intended to improve safety!

The first warnings of danger were given in the control room (top right) at the Chernobyl nuclear power plant (middle). The explosion happened in the reactor beside the tall chimney in the top lefthand corner of the picture. After the accident, helicopters (bottom) were used to spray the buildings with lead, clay, limestone and sand to put out the fire.

First reactions

Police and fire services rushed to the burning station. A policeman described it later:

'Near the bridge the car drove into either fog or dust – nothing could be seen over two metres and we drove blind. Bitumen drifted from the half-destroyed building of the fourth energy block, flames swirled above, people rushed. Near the main office building 'speedies' (ambulancemen) almost at a run were carrying someone on a stretcher. We found the doctor of the plant but he shrugged his shoulders.'

The local people asleep in their beds knew nothing of this as the power station was some kilometres away. As the deadly radioactive dust fell on to the villages and towns round about on the Friday, Saturday and Sunday, people carried on their lives as usual. The authorities told them nothing. Two women describe what happened on Monday. Mothers were asked to collect the children from school unexpectedly early. They had been told to get ready to leave Chernobyl. One mother said:

'I found my husband at home. The workers at his factory, he said, were told to get ready to evacuate Chernobyl with their families. We looked at each other terrified and we embraced each other. Only at that moment did we have the sensation of catastrophe.'

Another woman learned about the accident from a neighbour:

'I asked her what is was all about. She said there was a big accident at the power station and that I should leave immediately if I wanted to survive . . . They tried to hide the facts. Quite simply they wanted to conceal the scale of the accident.'

Buildings in the village near the Chernobyl nuclear power station were hosed down after the accident to try to remove radioactive fallout.

The levels of radioactivity on contaminated farmland were checked with Geiger counters.

A deadly cloud

The radioactive cloud which the explosion produced began to spread on the upper winds, blowing from the southeast into other parts of Europe. The first that people knew about it in the western European countries was late Saturday and early Sunday, in Sweden. Here the devices to detect radiation in the country's atomic power stations began to sound the alarm. The Swedish engineers thought the power stations had all developed faults at the same time, and were mystified. They soon realised that the radioactive dust was coming from outside the plants, not inside. By the end of the next week huge areas of Europe were experiencing fallout from the cloud. The worst of this fallout was in those areas where rain fell, washing out the materials: the heavier the rain, the worse the contamination.

In Britain heavy rain in the hills of parts of Wales, the Lake District and parts of Scotland produced high contamination of the thin hill soils. Plants soon took up the radioactive chemicals. The sheep eating these plants became contaminated but some were sold before scientists could monitor all the land. This means that the meat probably entered the shops and contaminated the people who ate it. In 1997 there were farms where the sheep were still receiving radiation from the fallout in the soils and could not be sold. In northern Sweden, the dangerous radioactive chemicals were taken up especially by plants named lichens. The lichens are food for reindeer herds on which the Saami (Lapp) people of the area depend for meat. In 1990 the contamination of the herds had become so bad that the Swedish government ordered many of them to be destroyed. A way of life that had lasted for centuries is now virtually wiped out in northern Sweden.

The aftermath

What happened on 25 April 1986 showed up the worst and some of the best in people. Although the officials were later prosecuted for their criminal negligence in running the plant, many of those who carried out the experiment so carelessly were either dead or would die later from radiation poisoning. Also to die later were many of the firemen who so bravely fought the fire. Even the helicopter pilots who flew again and again to within 200 metres of the fire to 'bomb' it with over 3000 tonnes of lead, limestone, clay and sand to put it out are now sick and dying. These were enormously brave people who sacrificed themselves to prevent the disaster becoming worse. In the early stages, for example, it looked as if the fire might spread to the other reactors. If they had been destroyed as well, even larger areas of the USSR could have been made uninhabitable. Only the bravery of the firefighters prevented it. They were true heroes.

Nobody knows yet how many people will die an early death as a result of Chernobyl. The radiation is widespread. About three million people live in the area of worst contamination. The worst affected are children. As one Ukrainian official said:

'At first the Soviet authorities did not tell us what was happening and we could not find out the extent of it because we had no equipment to monitor it. Now we can see it in ourselves. All the children in the contaminated areas have swollen thyroids. They do not laugh or run and play like children. They sit around in groups like old men.'

Even in 1997 children not born at the time of the disaster are now getting sick with swollen thyroid glands and radiation sickness and hospitals find it difficult to cope.

Chernobyl helped to destroy the USSR.

Those against

Chernobyl was not the first serious nuclear accident. In Britain there was one in 1957 which contaminated the land around a nuclear power station. Few people realised how serious it was outside the nuclear industry. In 1979 an accident took place in the USA very similar to Chernobyl but without its awful results.

The accident was at a plant called Three Mile Island in Pennsylvania. At 4am on 28 March a

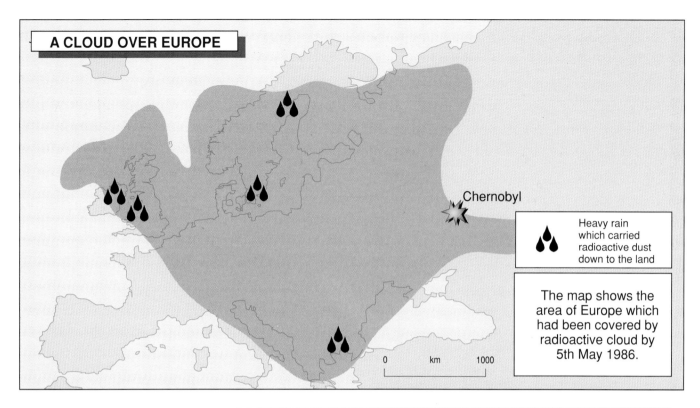

A CLOUD OVER EUROPE

Chernobyl

Heavy rain which carried radioactive dust down to the land

The map shows the area of Europe which had been covered by radioactive cloud by 5th May 1986.

0   km   1000

valve controlling the cooling water to the reactor suddenly shut down through a fault. The operators attempted to open it again but made a number of errors. As at Chernobyl, the reactor core was exposed to superheated steam and this discharged into the reactor building. Hydrogen, a very explosive gas, had formed in the steam and could have blown up the plant. Fortunately it was controlled and dispersed and the radioactivity in the steam cloud never reached the atmosphere outside the plant. Unlike at Chernobyl, the civil authorities alerted the people living in a five-mile radius. Plans were made to move about 2,400 people. To the astonishment of the authorities 144,000 people fled with many more fleeing who lived outside the five-mile distance. As one man said:

'They said we'd be OK but what the heck do they know. I just got my family in the car and went like a bat out of hell. No way was I staying round to find out.'

This accident stopped the whole nuclear power development in the USA. At the time President Carter was set to approve many new plants. These were cancelled. It took six years to make the Three Mile Island plant completely safe, at a cost of over one billion dollars. Since 1979 no new nuclear power stations have been built.

In Britain, nuclear power development has been suspended. The government has decided that electricity from nuclear power is too expensive to produce when the cost of dismantling the nuclear power plant is taken into account. The cost of dismantling Britain's oldest power stations was estimated at nearly £8 billion in 1994. By 1997 this was seen as probably too low as the cost of dismantling the later ones has been put between £40 billion and £100 billion.

Sweden has also abandoned its nuclear power station programme and Australia, Iceland, Nor

way, Luxemburg, Portugal, New Zealand and Ireland have all said they will not use nuclear power. It is likely that all these countries will spend much more in future on power production from sources such as sunlight, the waves, wind, natural gas and burning wastes. They will also do much more to conserve energy. These countries have passed the turning point towards energy conservation and non-pollution from nuclear power. Other countries have still to reach it.

The Future

Some countries still favoured nuclear power in spite of Chernobyl in the ten years after the accident. These were France, Germany, Belgium, and Japan. By 1997 however, most of these countries were changing their attitude. For instance, France (which produces 70 per cent of its electricity by nuclear power) in 1997 was not planning to build any more nuclear plants and had decided to build coal-fired power stations as well as developing more non-polluting sources of power such as the wind, Sun, the tides, hot rocks and running water. Only Japan of these countries still has an active nuclear programme for the next century. They plan to build 30–40 nuclear power stations. The Japanese argue that accidents like Three Mile Island or Chernobyl cannot happen again. They also say nuclear power is cheaper than other sources of power and does not produce greenhouse gases like burning coal, oil or natural gas.

Some East European countries are also dependent on nuclear power but many of their designs are old ones like that at Chernobyl. Countries like Bulgaria, Ukraine and the Czech Republic are seeking help from western countries to make them more safe.

Power stations are not the worst nuclear polluters. It is the old nuclear bomb-making factories in the USA and the former USSR which are worse. For instance, in the USA in 1994 the government admitted that 1377 places around the country had nuclear waste contamination from bomb-making. How to deal with wastes like these and from power stations is a big problem.

The Saami (Lapps), in northern Europe, were forced to slaughter most of their reindeer after the Chernobyl accident, The animals feed on lichens, which were heavily contaminated by radioactive fallout.

A history lesson

At present most nuclear wastes are stored in water-filled silos or shallow pits above ground. But some wastes are highly radioactive and very dangerous. They cannot be allowed to come into contact with the air or with water in the ground, so shallow burial is not possible. (When the USSR tried to store nuclear wastes in this way a huge explosion in their dump in the Ural Mountains scattered them far and wide in the 1950s. The Russians told nobody. It was only detected when migrating birds from that region arrived in the Mediterranean area and were found to be highly contaminated.) As the radioactivity of some of these wastes can be very long-lasting, some will remain dangerous for thousands of years.

Various solutions have been proposed to deal with the most dangerous wastes. One is to turn them into a sort of glass, a process named vitrification. The radioactive chemicals are held apart from each other in the glass, so heat cannot build up. The radiation they produce will be absorbed by the glassy materials so only a small amount will escape. The glass itself will not rot like concrete or metal. So far this solution is only at an experimental stage. The most common idea is to bury the wastes deep underground, encased in strong metal containers. As water circulates underground, these containers must be made so that they will not rot. They will have to last for thousands of years. Do we know whether metals can last this long without rotting?

To find out, scientists are now studying closely what has happened to ancient metal. For example, just after the Roman armies came to Britain in the first century AD, they invaded what is now Scotland and set up camps. Eventually they abandoned these camps but in one they hid and buried about two tonnes of iron nails. Perhaps they wanted to use these when they returned. They never came back, so the nails lay buried in the soil for nealy 2000 years until archaeologists dug them up a few

Low-level radioactive wastes are usually buried in shallow pits (below left), but it could be safer to turn them into a kind of glass (below).

Bronze Age armour may provide clues that will help scientists to make containers for nuclear waste that will last for thousands of years.

This basalt cave, near Washington in the USA, could be used to house nuclear wastes. Basalt is a very hard rock with few cracks, so little water seeps in.

years ago. The archaeologists were amazed to find that the nails had hardly rotted at all. Some on the outside were rusty on the surface. However, the nails inside the pile were as good as new. This was in spite of water from the soil having trickled through the pile for all that time. The Roman iron was so pure that it did not rust. The iron and steel we make now rust because they are not pure.

Similar evidence comes from Sweden. The cannons made from bronze (copper and tin) which were carried by Swedish warships and sunk 400 years ago near the shore, showed that only the first millimetre or so of metal had been affected by the salty seawater. Even older metals for the Greek bronze age armour of the kind worn by the soldiers of Athens and Troy are being studied. Scientists believe that all these studies will give them clues so that they can make safe atomic waste containers to store underground.

The arguments for and against nuclear power will go on for many years to come. Steering industry in new directions is not easy. It is hoped that we all take part in the process. The people at Chernobyl never had the choice.

CHAPTER FIVE

MORE PEOPLE, MORE POLLUTION

At present the world's population is rising rapidly. By 2020 there will be about 7000 million people in the world, nearly 1½ billion more than now. The industries that produce the chemicals for farming argue that we will need huge amounts of extra food to feed everybody. So chemicals will be needed in even larger quantities than now. This seems like a good argument. But against it we know that modern intensive farming is already damaging the planet. Adding even more pollution will affect the world's climate, which will eventually harm the farming we rely on. So are we trapped between the choices of letting people starve in order to reduce the pollution or increasing industrialised farming and creating more pollution? The simple answer is no. We can increase food supplies and repair the damage caused by pollution.

Factory food

The photograph on the opposite page shows a new kind of 'farm'. It looks like a chemical factory, which in fact is what it is. But instead of producing chemicals for industrial goods, it produces a number of chemicals that can be used as food. One of them is a white powder which is pure protein. The cattle in front of this plant are fed on a mixture of this powder, grass and an artificial 'hay', which is made mainly of waste paper. The cattle thrive on this diet. The chemicals are not only suitable as cattle feed. They can be textured and flavoured and have vitamins added so that they become a complete food for people as well. The raw material for making these foods is a liquid named methanol, which is made from waste products of the oil industry. The company that owns this factory claims that with two such factories they could produce enough protein to replace all the meat eaten in Britain.

This factory is at the beginning of a whole new technology which uses biological processes (biotechnology) to produce foods. Microscopic plants (bacteria and fungi) are collected in the wild and taken to the laboratory. Then biologists use genetic engineering to alter the bacteria and fungi, so that these tiny plants will feed on substances such as methanol and turn it into food.

Seeds that have been genetically altered are preserved in a seed bank.

The factory in the background makes an artificial food, which the cows feed on.

Genetic engineering is a way of altering the chemistry of a living thing in a permanent way. All living things have chemical instructions in their cells, named genes, which tell the cells what to do. Genetic engineering alters these instructions so that, for example, the bacteria and fungi can grow on materials which are different from those on which they feed in the wild.

There are many other foods which could be made using bacteria and fungi and industrial raw materials such as oil and gas. In fact, it would be possible to exist completely on artificially-produced foods.

Nitrates mean more food

Just over 100 years ago, biologists learned how plants feed themselves and what the soil must contain for plants to grow successfully. Green plants take water, and chemicals named minerals from the soil. The minerals include nitrogen, iron, phosphorus, magnesium, calcium, potassium and sulphur. Biologists call these minerals nutrients. It was also discovered that more nitrogen was needed than other nutrients.

Nitrogen is all around us in the form of a gas in the air. But plants can only absorb nitrogen

from the soil, joined to other chemicals such as hydrogen and oxygen. These combined forms are named nitrates. Nitrates get into the soil in a number of ways, from lightning flashes to animal droppings. Chemists found that if large extra quantities of nitrates were put on the soil, crop yields could be increased dramatically. They set about finding ways to make the nitrates in factories. By the 1920s the first fertiliser factories had appeared and fertiliser manufacture soon became a major industry.

Nitrates: a threat to health

To increase crop yields nitrates have been put on to the land in such amounts in the last 20 years that the crops cannot use it all. Much of it is washed off the land by rain and enters the streams and rivers or sinks into the ground and dissolves into underground water. In many places in western Europe and the USA nitrate has become a dangerous pollutant. In fact, in many of these countries farming now produces more river pollution than industry.

Nitrates are dangerous for two main reasons. First, they are poisonous and can cause cancer in people. Secondly, the wild plants in the rivers take up the nitrates just as the crops do. Some

Nodules on the roots of the broad bean contain bacteria which make nitrates.

The reeds in marshes beside rivers help to soak up fertilisers that drain into the water.

wild plants, such as algae (simple green plants) can grow so much that they smother other plants and even use up all the oxygen in the water. Fish and other animals may suffocate. One type of algae, blue-green algae, can also produce very poisonous compounds. One of these is even more poisonous than cobra venom! Officially in Britain over 400 lakes and ponds are affected by blue-green algae, including some drinking water reservoirs. In Finland and Russia people have died from eating fish poisoned by these plants.

Some rivers have been altered to improve land drainage and this has made the problem of algae growth worse. This happened to the river Skjer in Denmark during the 1980s. Before this, much of the nitrate and other fertilisers were soaked up by marshes growing in the bends of the river. Then the river was straightened and the marshes removed to create more farmland. The fertilisers could no longer be soaked up by the marsh plants and the river life was suffocated by the rapid growth of algae. The Danish government now intends to put all the bends back again so that new marshes can grow. In Florida there are similar plans to conserve the marshes of the Everglades so they can soak up fertilisers, and Sweden intends to encourage marsh plant growth as well.

Biological control

The water cleaning by the marshes of the river Skjer is an example of biological control. That is, using Nature's own weapons to fight pollution. There are likely to be many other examples in future. For instance, the continent of Australia is bracing itself to fight off an invasion. During the last decade a deadly enemy of cattle has been slowly migrating across the island of New Guinea towards Australia. This is the screw worm fly which lays its eggs in the skin of cattle. When the grubs hatch they feed on the animal flesh and produce bad sores on the skin. These then become infected with other diseases. To counter the screw worm fly, biological defences are being prepared. These are other male screw

worm flies which are being bred in millions. They have one important difference to the future invader: they have been sterilised. They can mate with a normal female fly but the female cannot lay fertile eggs. Thus it is hoped that the population of screw worm flies will die out quickly. This method has been tried and tested in the southern USA, where it was very successful. Methods of biological control like this can eliminate the need for expensive polluting insecticides.

At a simpler level, in Thailand, in the drier, poorer parts of the country, many fish are bred and live in the rice paddies (flooded fields). The fish keep down insect pests by eating their grubs in the water. They consume the seeds of weedy plants and even eat manure – animal and human – produced by the farms. Biological control has been developed as a cheap, effective substitute for expensive insecticides. The Thai agricultural service has introduced new fish, in addition to the traditional carp, which grow quickly on the diet of wastes, insect grubs and weedy plants. The scheme is so effective, and makes such a good profit from the fish-selling that farmers in the richer regions want to use it as well. Unfortunately, they will not be able to do so for a number of years as they were encouraged to use lots of herbicides and

Some rice farmers raise fish in their flooded fields. The fish help to keep the water clean, so the rice grows better.

insecticides in the past. These chemicals have polluted the paddies and it will take some years to make them clean enough for fish to live in.

Controlling insect pests and weeds using only small amounts of chemicals and relying more on biological control is being researched and encouraged now in Malaysia and the Philippines as well as Thailand.

Biologists are also trying to produce crops which can make their own fertiliser, just as peas and beans can. If the genes of crops such as maize, wheat, barley and soya beans can be changed to do this, then less nitrate fertiliser will be needed. Some strains of rice produce their own chemical defences through their roots against weeds and leaves against insects. It is hoped that these can be bred from to reduce the need for chemicals even more.

Safe to eat?

'An apple a day keeps the doctor away' is an old saying. Is it as true as it was? Apples, like most fruit and vegetables, are sprayed with chemicals to keep down pests (insects, fungi and weeds). Many fruits are also sprayed with chemicals to preserve them while in storage.

Much of the chemicals have disappeared by the time we eat the food. However, in 1988–89 one out of every two apples officially tested in Britain still had remains of the chemicals either on the skin or inside the fruit. All these chemicals have been tested and passed as safe for people to eat at the levels found in food when eaten. But as we may eat these remains over many years, there is no way of knowing what the long-term harm might be.

Cooking vegetables can change the remains of the chemicals. For instance, tests have shown that of three chemicals in sprayed potatoes, cooking actually *increased* one of them. After peeling and boiling there was 60 per cent more of the chemical, and after baking 600 per cent more.

Because people are now worried about the use of so many chemicals on food, steps are being taken to use much less of them. For example, the USA is quick to ban or restrict any chemicals which laboratory tests show to cause cancer in animal experiments. The Dutch and Danish authorities are also very vigilant. They have cut the use of pesticides by half since 1990. This level has already been reached in Sweden, which has the most advanced programme for cutting chemicals.

Cutting down on chemicals does not necessarily mean that yields and profits will be cut. In Sweden, the cutting of chemicals is combined with organic farming (using only natural manures and no sprays), crop rotations so weeds cannot get a hold on any one field, and very efficient spraying equipment. The food yields are the same and the farm profits are greater as less has to be spent on sprays and spraying.

It is very likely that such methods will dominate farming in the rich countries in the next decade. One American study of the growth of organic farming suggests that half of all food will be free of artificial chemicals by 2020. In Europe, the countries of the European Union are likely to adopt the Dutch and Danish targets in the next few years.

Most fruit (left) is sprayed with chemicals.

Mixed farming (right), where animal manures are used to help fertilise the soil, is much less polluting than farming that relies solely on chemicals.

CHAPTER SIX

DESIGNS FOR THE FUTURE

'Where there's muck, there's money.' The people who coined this phrase lived in the towns in northern England which grew with the Industrial Revolution. The people had no choice but to put up with dirty air, poor housing, industrial litter and polluted rivers for the sake of the money that was made from the new industries. People are now less willing to accept the 'muck'. They want a clean, safe environment for their children to grow up in. Muck and money do not have to go together.

Clean and efficient

The countries of western Europe and some places in the USA now have strong laws against certain kinds of pollution. In addition, much of the worst pollution caused by industry and its products has gone because of changes in industry itself. To many engineers in the advanced industrial countries pollution is now a sign of bad design and inefficiency.

In all the major world car factories engineers are busy experimenting with new engines. Some of these are made of materials such as the very hard pottery first used in the Space vehicles of the USA. Others are improving the diesel engine. In some cities in Germany and Holland there are now very low inner city speed limits, to make motor vehicles travel at the same speed as bicycles. These new limits will reduce pollution and prevent accidents,

Sunraycer crossed Australia and won the first international race for solar-powered cars in 1987. The use of solar energy and other renewable energy sources reduces pollution.

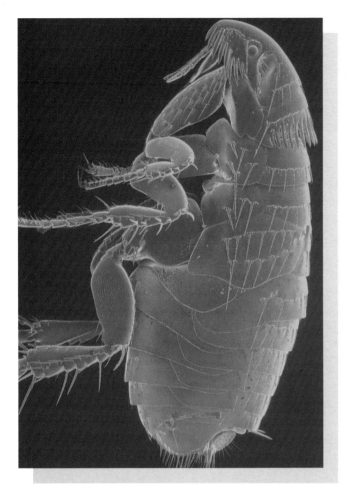

The tiny flea can leap many times its own height. Engineers would like to be able to imitate the efficient way the flewa stores and releases large amounts of energy.

saving money as well as lives. Vehicles to suit these limits will include combined electric- and diesel-powered cars (as well as trolley buses and trams). The electric motor will be used in the town and the diesel outside, when the batteries will be recharged. In 1994 an American car maker entered a 'green' car in the famous 24 hour Le Mans race. It used gas turbine, flywheel and electricity for power.

Most car makers are also trying to find ways of reducing the friction (rubbing) of many moving parts. We know that if a car could be designed with friction-free bearings, its fuel consumption would drop by half immediately. Some oil companies are experimenting with algae which can produce clean, oil-like fuel.

If all these experiments are successful, a lot of the pollution will be designed out of industry and its products. In fact, all these ideas and experiments add up to another industrial revolution. Just as there is a conservation revolution taking place in agriculture, so there is an even more exciting one beginning in industry.

In the twenty-first century the watchword of industry will not be 'Where there's muck, there's money' but another old saying, 'Waste not, want not'.

Corals and chemical engineering

Animals and plants have some very ingenious answers to chemical and engineering problems. If we can unlock some of Nature's secrets we could use them to improve the efficiency of our machines, chemical processes and many of our industrial products. As efficiency increased, pollution would decrease.

Corals have lived in the oceans for hundreds of millions of years. They are obviously highly successful animals. Yet they often live in waters which have very little of the materials they need to grow. The coral animal needs lots of a chemical named phosphate, which is taken from the sea water around it. Yet the tropical waters in which the corals live very often have hardly any of this mineral in them. How the coral manages to obtain so much phosphate has long puzzled biologists. It was always assumed that the coral had some very special chemical process for this. Biologists have looked for such a process in the animal and not found one.

When Australian engineers began to study the Great Barrier Reef in the 1980s to see how it could be conserved, they realised the coral was doing something impossible in even the most advanced chemical industry. It was taking phosphate from the sea water ten times more efficiently than any factory could. It became clear that it was not the chemistry alone that allowed the coral to do this. It was the detailed shape of the coral. The surface of the coral is engineered to increase the extraction rate. The surface form of the coral is what mathematicians name a 'fractal' surface (see photograph on the next page). It is a series of repeating shapes which get smaller and smaller, right down to levels that can only be seen with a microscope. If the surface was flattened out it would cover an enormous area. It is this huge surface area which allows the coral to take out so much phosphate.

The mathematics of fractals have only been worked out in the last twenty years. Now that its effectiveness has been shown in the coral, there are many chemical processes which could benefit from it. For instance, the battery in a car uses sheets of metal to interact with the acid to produce a current. If these sheets of metal had fractal surfaces, the output and life of the battery could be extended many times. This would reduce battery sizes and make efficient, long-distance electric vehicles a very real possibility. Another use would be for extracting wastes like metals from water. At present much of the valuable dissolved metals and other chemicals from industry are poured into rivers, which carry them eventually to the sea. This is a waste of materials and money. With fractal surface extractors, the metal could be taken out of the water even at very low concentrations. In fact, all kinds of pollutants could be removed from liquids much more efficiently.

In future, the scientists and engineers together will uncover many more natural processes which can help us.

The complex patterns of corals (below), and fractals (inset, on a computer) may help engineers to design machines that will extract pollutants from water.

In the future, rivers polluted with mercury (right) and other heavy metals may be cleaned by adding acorns (above), ground to a powder. Acorns contain a chemical that attracts heavy metals, so areas with large numbers of oak trees could clean up their waterways.

Small is beautiful

Another industrial design change that can lessen pollution is the reduction in the amounts of materials needed to make and run machines. The development of the microchip has reduced the demand for materials. The transmission of information by thin glass wires (fibre optics), where the signal is a light pulse, is reducing the demand for metals for heavy cables in telephone systems and cable TV, and there are many other examples.

Making things lighter, stronger and more efficient is the result of new discoveries about chemicals. For instance, the chemical commonly used to make microchips is silicon. This is quite good at doing the job but newer materials now exist which may be even better. Gallium arsenide, for example, is much more sensitive to light than silicon and is better at generating electric current from sunlight. In 1990 a glider-like aeroplane flew right across the USA in 40 days. It was powered by sunlight converted to electricity by gallium arsenide embedded in a plastic film which coated the body and wings. Another discovery was that plastic can be made to transmit electricity if it has certain impurities added such as iodine. This accidental discovery is being researched to provide a cheap alternative to heavy metal cables. Again, pollution levels will fall as the use of metals is reduced.

As machines and equipment get lighter, they also get smaller. As less materials are needed to do a particular job, so the pollutants from the manufacturing processes are reduced. As many of these machines also need less energy to run them, the demand for power falls. Most industrial countries forecast their energy needs so that they can plan new power stations. Since these countries began to do this about 40 years ago, all the forecasts have been proved wrong. Although the industrial output grew, the forecasts were always for more power than was actually needed. If the forecasts of 40 years ago had been right then the levels of pollution would now be far worse than they actually are. New materials and design have done more to reduce pollution from this source than any legal restrictions on air pollution.

CHAPTER SEVEN

WORLD PROBLEMS
WORLD SOLUTIONS

About 120 years ago, the first warnings were published by scientists on what is now called 'the greenhouse effect'. The danger was seen to be that some of the gases being added to the atmosphere by industry and vehicles would trap heat being radiated from the Earth and the atmosphere would warm up. This would lead to melting of glacier ice and a rise of sea levels. These gases – carbon dioxide, methane, nitrous oxide and others – let radiation from the Sun through but they absorb radiation from the Earth. (They act a bit like the glass in a greenhouse.) Many scientists (but not all) think that this is now happening. In 1990 they persuaded many governments to agree with them so that limits on the release of greenhouse gases would be imposed. At first some indust-rialised countries did not agree the problem was very serious but by 1997 they were convinced. In that year most of the world's countries were ready to sign an agreement to reduce their release of greenhouse gases especially carbon dioxide. They will impose limits on vehicles, power stations, all kinds of industry and agriculture. It is now up to science and engineering to match these limits.

Sea level is rising now (1997) at about 2 millimetres per year. But if ice, especially from the huge ice sheets of West Antarctica, begins to melt quickly as the seas and air warm up, many

Pollution levels can be monitored from Space. This false-colour satellite picture shows where plants are growing. On the land, the green areas have most plants and the yellow areas have the least. In the sea, red indicates most plants and pink the least.

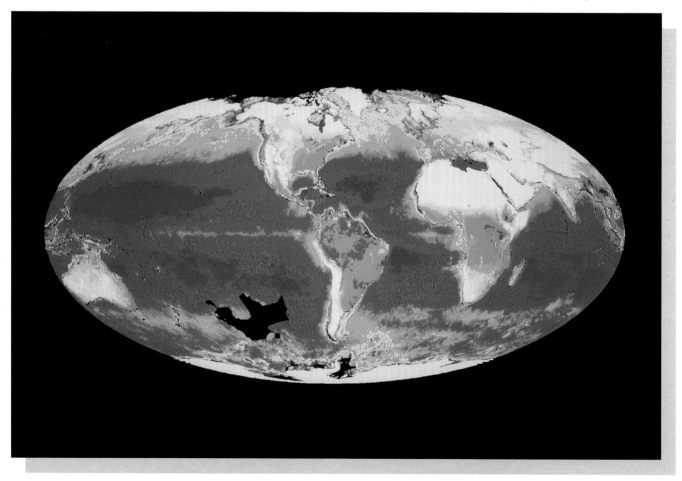

scientists think the sea will rise much faster. By 2100 AD many think it might have risen by one metre; others say much less. But most are agreed weather is likely to become windier and stormier as pollution makes the oceans and air heat up.

The greenhouse threat

New energy sources and new manufacturing methods will help to reduce the greenhouse effect. For example, at present there are 20,000 wind-powered electricity generators in California as well as a number of solar-powered electricity producers. As the technology of renewable energy becomes more efficient, and the electricity it produces becomes cheaper, there will be a switch over from fossil fuels to renewable energy. Already a new kind of solar furnace has been designed which will give temperatures higher than the Sun's surface itself if we need them. In Britain, in 1994 the government promised to help develop a number of renewable energy power sources. These include wind, rubbish burning and gas from waste heaps but it has dropped its support for wave power and hot rock power. Many scientists think this is not a sensible policy.

Methane gas can be used to raise steam and drive a turbine to generate electricity. The gas, which normally escapes into the air, is collected from a waste dump. This power station is in California, USA.

Hot rocks, for example, has great possibilities all round the world. There are huge reserves of heat from the inside of the Earth which could be tapped as it is now in Iceland, New Zealand, USA, Mexico, Italy and other countries. Many poor countries in Asia, Africa and South America have volcanoes and could produce their electric power from Earth heat. By 2020, in any case, about one fifth of all the world's power will be produced by hydro-electric plants. None of these sources adds to the greenhouse effect.

Turning down the fires

As machines become more efficient, the burning of fossil fuels will gradually disappear. Much of the wastes we throw away now will be fuelling specially-built power stations. Five power stations in the USA are already fuelled by old car tyres (the smoke is not allowed to escape), and a new one is planned for Britain. Many stations are now being designed to use gas turbine engines where the hot gases are also used for heating. The factories shown on page

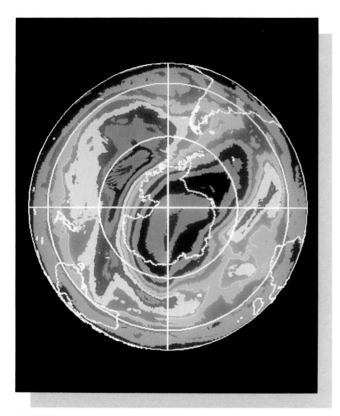

The 'hole' in the ozone layer is shown on this false-colour satellite map as deep blue, purple, black and grey.

21 will now have their own 1750 MW generator using this combined power and heat system. The gas which fuels it is collected from all parts of the plant. The gases used to be burned off wastefully in the atmosphere. Power could also be produced from town and farm wastes. In Britain and the USA, methane gas from old buried waste dumps is collected to provide power. A small power station in Britain will even burn chicken manure.

The greenhouse effect can also be limited by planting trees. Gases produced in industrial countries can be absorbed by trees far away in developing countries, and the people there can make use of the new forests. Power companies in the northeast USA have developed a scheme to plant millions of trees in Guatemala to soak up the extra carbon dioxide produced by the fuel in their new power stations. This scheme has been joined by the authorities of Toronto in Canada. So far about 80 million trees have been planted. A similar scheme has been developed in Holland to plant trees in Indonesia.

Recycling waste materials will also reduce pollution. Aluminium, glass, paper and now plastic are becoming widely re-used. Now that the problems of pollution are better under-

stood, we can begin to repair the damage already done and limit any more damage. In fact, the task of repair is already under way.

Pollution protocol

In 1987 for the first time, the polluting countries of the world agreed to cooperate in reducing a single threat from the pollution they have created. These countries signed a document named the Montreal Protocol. In it they agreed to reduce the production of gases named chlorofluorocarbons, or CFCs. Other poorer countries like India and China have joined the Protocol as well. In 1990 they all agreed to speed up the process and by 1997 very little CFCs were being used or released.

The reasons why CFCs are seen to be special is that they are destroying the layer of gas named ozone which surrounds the Earth in the high atmosphere. High flying jumbo jets and rockets also help to destroy it. CFCs have been used widely for many years as coolant fluid in refrigerators, to expand plastic foams and to propel gases from aerosol cans. Many tonnes have been released. At ground level they do little harm, but when they reach the upper air the chlorine in them attacks and breaks down the gas ozone. This is a special form of oxygen. Ozone absorbs ultra-violet rays from the Sun and keeps them from the plants and animals on the Earth which could be harmed by them. Ultra-violet rays cause skin and eye defects in people and animals and harm the small green plants in the oceans – the plankton. They also tan the skin of white people. By 1997, scientists had found not only that many kinds of amphibians (frogs, toads and newts) were beginning to disappear around the world but some frogs were turning bright orange from UV light. Their thin skins needed for breathing make them very vunerable to damaging UV rays from the Sun.

Sea control

Some of the worst pollution problems are now building up in the world's seas. As the industrial countries pour chemical wastes into them the living things are being poisoned. So far it is the

Dinosaurs: victims of pollution?

Until 65 million years ago, dinosaurs had ruled the world unchallenged for over 100 million years. Then they suddenly disappeared. Until recently, nobody has been able to explain what happened to make them so suddenly become extinct.

About 25 years ago, as more and more rocks around the world were studied it became clear that the dinosaurs were not the only animals to die out at that time. Many marine animals also disappeared. In fact, it began to look as if almost half the animal species had suddenly vanished at about the same time, 65 million years ago.

Careful study of the minerals in the rocks of that age found a layer which contained a rare chemical named iridium. This layer appeared to exist in many different parts of the world, even though it was in different kinds of rocks. Some geologists concluded it must have fallen from the air into the sea and sunk to the bottom where the rocks were forming. Most geologists agree that the iridium was the result of a collision between the Earth and a gigantic meteorite.

Large objects hit the Earth every 1000 years or so. A small comet blew up over Tunguska in Siberia in 1908, for example, with the force of 12 million tonnes of TNT – 12 megatonnes. The one which hit Yucatan in Mexico 65 million years ago was the size of a large mountain at least 10 kilometres in diameter. The shock of the collision would have instantly killed all life on a continent the size of Asia. The dust and gas pollution thrown into the sky would have cut off the sunlight right round the Earth for years cooling the climate and killing many kinds of land and marine plant and animal life, including all the dinosaurs. At the same time huge volcanic eruptions in India also added to pollution of the atmosphere. Of the backboned animals on land only a few kinds of birds, reptiles, amphibians and mammals survived. All of the land animals now have evolved from these – including us! We are the lucky survivors of this pollution disaster long ago. Some people say the pollution we are creating now might make us follow the dinosaurs if we do nothing about it soon!

seas close to the industrial countries themselves but the pollution is beginning to appear in marine creatures far from the industrial regions. The countries around the North Sea and the Mediterranean have now agreed that this situation cannot go on. They have set up organisations to measure and control the pollution so that the seas become cleaner. This is not just to help themselves. The tiny plants in the oceans are one of the main ways carbon dioxide is taken out of the air, so if they are damaged the greenhouse effect could get worse. Already other plants which absorb carbon dioxide are being destroyed in large numbers as the tropical rainforests are cut down and burned.

Eventually it is likely that the whole of the world's oceans will have to be saved from pollution. We have the technology to do this as we can see what the worst effects are and where they are happening by using satellites (see photograph on page 40). Or we can use other kinds of ingenious schemes like that set up by American researchers in the Southern Ocean.

This generates sound waves in the water which will be picked up around the world. The sound waves will travel along deeper bands of cold water in the ocean depths. Any change of speed will show that a change of temperature is taking place.

Unfortunately, this noise is itself another kind of pollution. In 1997 scientists began to recognize that ocean-going ships were making the seas very noisy and some of the biggest ships might be affecting marine life, for instance, the large whales which rely a lot on sound for communication.

As you can see from the material in this book, pollution is not as hopeless a problem as it is sometimes stated to be. The most important stage of repairing the damage from pollution is getting a clear idea of exactly what is happening but to make use of what we know, it needs ordinary people – including children – to be involved. We are the first generation of the Age of Conservation.

GLOSSARY

bacteria – a group of single-celled plants growing in all environments. Some can cause disease but most are essential to the ecology of the planet.

biotechnology – the use of bacteria or other living organisms to benefit people (eg to treat water or waste, or to produce food).

biological control – the use of living organisms to control other, damaging organisms.

colonisation – the process in which plants or animals move into a new environment and become established.

DDT – dichlorodiphenyltrichloroethane, which is used as an insecticide.

ecology – the study of how plants, animals and people are related to their environment.

environment – the surroundings in which plants and animals live and which provide them with what they need to live.

false-colour satellite picture – a satellite picture coloured in by a computer, which does not show the true colours but which shows up certain features of the land or sea in bright, strong colours.

food chain – a group of organisms, each of which feeds on another and is itself eaten by an organism higher up the chain. The first organism in any food chain is a plant.

fungi – a group of plants without green colour which feed on dead or living plant or animal matter.

intensive farming – farming that involves the use of large quantities of chemicals to increase crop yields and meat production.

Old Stone Age – (also called Palaeolithic) from about three million years ago until about 12 000 BC. Early people used simple, unpolished stone tools.

HAMILTON COLLEGE

INDEX